THE FAITH OF THE PRESIDENTS

THE FAITH
OF THE
PRESIDENTS

Compiled and written by Anne E. Schraff
Illustrated by Don Kueker

Publishing House
St. Louis

Concordia Publishing House, St. Louis, Missouri
Copyright © 1978 Concordia Publishing House

MANUFACTURED IN THE UNITED STATES OF AMERICA

Library of Congress Cataloging in Publication Data

Schraff, Anne E.
        The faith of the Presidents.

        (Christian heroes)
        SUMMARY: Sketches of ten Presidents focusing on inspirational moments in their lives.
            1. Presidents—United States—Religion—Juvenile literature. 2. Presidents—United States—
Biography—Juvenile literature. (1. Presidents—Religion)
I. Title.   II. Series.
E176.8.S35   973'.0992 (B)   77-28723
ISBN 0-570-07877-6
ISBN 0-570-07882-2 pbk.

To all my students at OLP who shared with me the Good News about Jesus and with special thanks to Betty Yip who assisted me in the research on James Garfield.

Contents

Prolog

In the following stories the religious faith of 10 presidents is shown as a guiding force in their lives. Some, like James Garfield, Benjamin Harrison, and William McKinley had at one time considered the ministry as a full-time career. Many, like Garfield and McKinley, had come forth in their young lives to publicly commit themselves to Christ. John Quincy Adams for every day of his 81 years closed his eyes in sleep only after reciting the simple evening prayer, "Now I lay me down to sleep. . . ." Van Buren's religion was expressed not only in his joyous singing of hymns on Sunday, but even more eloquently in his concern for the forgotten poor of debtors prison. John Adams, along with his remarkable wife Abigail, believed that he was on earth to serve God and humanity. When his conscience directed him to make an unpopular but right decision, he explained simply, "Before God I had no choice."

After leaving office James Buchanan became a church member; throughout his life, with oustanding Christian charity, he cared for numerous nieces and nephews orphaned by the scourge of illness in his family. Chester Arthur, with a lifelong concern for the rights of minorities, not only attended his church but often other churches on the same Sunday. The dying John Tyler, after a life struck by illness and misfortune, called upon the faith of his childhood and had a bright and consoling encounter with Christ.

These men, as all humankind, had their failings and shortcomings. In their special trials, where they carried not only their own hopes and dreams but also the fate of the country they loved, they turned to God for strength. From the plain brown meeting house where John Adams worshiped, to the little Dutch church where Van Buren sang, to the icy fields of Valley Forge where a future president knelt in the snow, these men expressed their faith.

The question might be raised: Why have George Washington, Thomas Jefferson, and Abraham Lincoln, as well as all 20th-century presidents, been excluded from this anthology?

So much has been written about Washington, and (although he was an active member of the Episcopal Church) there is so much question about his religious views, that it was thought best not to have a chapter on him. As for the 20th-century presidents, it was felt that they are too close to us and therefore too controversial.

Jefferson and Lincoln, while they were men of great faith and were motivated by strong religious convictions, never professed the doctrines of the basic Christian creeds. Jefferson was definitely a deist, not a Christian. Lincoln seems to have come closer to Christianity in his later years, but he never publicly confessed Christ or joined a church. However, both men recognized the place of religious faith in the great task before them as presidents in times of great difficulty in our country's history.

Jefferson, a principal figure in the formulation of both the Declaration of Independence and the Bill of Rights, defended religious freedom and wrote: "I have sworn upon the altar of God eternal hostility against every form of tyranny over the mind of man. Almighty God hath created the mind free."

Lincoln, on the morning of Feb. 11, 1861, left Springfield, Ill., for the last time. From the rear platform of his train he said to his friends and neighbors:

> I now leave, not knowing when, or whether ever, I may return, with a task before me greater than that which rested upon Washington. Without the assistance of that Divine Being who ever attended him (Washington), I cannot succeed. With that assistance, I cannot fail. Trusting in Him who can go with me, and remain with you, and be everywhere for good, let us confidently hope that all will yet be well. To His care commending you, as I hope in your prayers you will commend me, I bid you an affectionate farewell. . . .

Lincoln, like American presidents before and after him, recognized the importance of faith in performing the awesome tasks of the president of the United States.

Of the 10 presidents whose stories are told in this book, all except James Madison were professing Christians. In their prayers and their worship they found the strength and the courage to lead America through times of peril. With them and like them, may we as a nation always look up and see the face of God.

Anne E. Schraff ∎

John Adams

SECOND PRESIDENT 1797-1801

1

Before God and His Conscience:
John Adams

There was a loud crash, and glass splintered into the room. Young Abigail Adams heard her youngest child cry out in fear, and she rushed to see if the baby was all right. "It's all right," she soothed the child. She went to the window and saw three young men, their faces distorted with hatred. "Traitors!" they screamed, "Defender of murderers! Where is the traitor Adams? Is he too cowardly to show his face?"

"Be off before I whip some manners into you," the slim girl cried angrily.

The boys were shocked to hear such fiery words from a young woman, and they hurried off into the darkness.

When Abigail's husband, John, returned later in the evening, he turned ashen at the sight of the vandalism. "Abigail, I cannot bear the thought that my actions have placed you and the children in peril!"

Abigail tossed her long dark hair, "I guess I am a match for a few ill-mannered boys! I surely will not have you violate your conscience over concern for me!"

John Adams could not help but smile and recall his first meeting with this spirited girl. He had known her since childhood, but he didn't really notice her until one special day. Perhaps that was because her sisters were prettier and livelier than she, or so it seemed. Abigail was a small, quiet girl whom nobody seemed to notice as she sat off to one side in the parlor, sewing or reading. She had serious brown eyes, ad she wore brown or gray dresses. She reminded John of a shy fawn in the forest, her dark hair framing her pale face, the candlelight glowing on her cheeks.

On this particular day John had approached the quiet girl and looked at the book in her hands. He had expected to find her reading pretty sonnets, but instead it was a thick book titled Human Understanding by none other than the famous philosopher John Locke. Why, this was difficult reading for university-trained men!

"My," said 26-year-old John Adams to the 17-year-old neighbor girl, "what a big book for such a little head."

John had expected she would shyly giggle and make some silly remark about the book, such as many girls of that time would. Perhaps she would admit she did not really understand the large, difficult words—and would John be so kind as to explain them?

But Abigail looked up sharply, her brown eyes afire, and she almost snapped, "Even a little head longs for knowledge!"

John was taken aback. He was sorry he had spoken to patronizingly to her. As time went by, he noticed that she read Shakespeare and philosophy as well as poetry, although she had never been to school. In those times it was considered foolish to give education to a girl even if she was bright. Abigail's parents did not approve of the girl reading books on philosophy, and it was hard for her to get her hands on these books. John Adams began to lend her books from his own library, and they started to have long, involved conversations on such matters as the meaning of life. John was delighted to notice how really beautiful Abigail was, and also that she was extremely intelligent.

14

"Abigail," he asked her one day, "what do you see as our purpose here on earth?"

"Men and women are here to serve God and humanity," Abigail said seriously. "We are accountable to God for every moment of our time. We are made in the image of God, and we must fulfill our promise or we are a blasphemy to God. An hour wasted is an hour's sin!"

John agreed heartily. He was overjoyed that this young lady, for whom he had begun to care, shared his own deeply held beliefs. The young couple began to see each other regularly, and John discovered that not only was Abigail the most religious young lady he had ever met, but also the most joyous and happy. She was like a bubbling waterfall, always laughing, always seeing the beauty of life. He often said of her, "She makes me so happy! No sour-faced girl who made everyone feel sad, her Christian beliefs made her ever a joy to know."

And now, as Abigail swept up the glass from the floor, once again those brown eyes laughed. John knew Abigail had given him the support he needed to follow the dictates of his conscience. Even rocks hurled through his window at night could not daunt Abigail. Even cries of "Traitor!" could not disturb her, not when she was sure John was right.

The incident that turned most of their friends against the Adamses was the so-called Boston Massacre. In 1770 a group of angry Bostonians began throwing snowballs at some British soldiers. The mood of the crowd turned ugly, and soon they were hurling sticks and stones at the frightened soldiers. Suddenly a British soldier fired, and during the terrible moments that followed, five Bostonians were killed. It was called a "massacre," and the entire city turned in bitter hatred against the British soldiers. They were arrested and put on trial for murder. The mood of Boston was so violent that no British lawyer would defend the British soldiers. A friend of the soldiers came to the young American lawyer John Adams and said, "As God is my witness, these men are innocent. They were only defending their lives from the mob. I beg you, Mr.

Adams, defend them. If you do not, then they shall be condemned to death for murder!"

John Adams was strongly sympathetic to the cause of the American colonists. Like many Americans, he felt the British were passing unjust laws, unfairly taxing the Americans, taking away their rights. John's own cousin, Samuel Adams, was leading a fiery group which denounced the Boston Massacre as sheer cold-blooded murder. John had seen with his own eyes the bloody shirts taken from the slain Bostonians being waved in the air by wild-eyed young men who swore vengeance.

John Adams knew that any American lawyer who defended the British soldiers risked the everlasting hatred of all his friends. He knew it could ruin his financial and political future forever. But he also felt that the British soldiers had acted in self-defense and were not guilty of murder. So he held out his hand to the man who came begging for his help and said, "If these men cannot have a fair trial without my help, then I shall give my help."

To Abigail, John explained his agonizingly hard decision, "Before God and my conscience I had no choice."

Abigail had agreed in an instant. She never once wavered as bitter abuse was heaped upon their heads. Ruffians smashed their windows, chanted ugly slogans at their doorstep and cured the Adams name. But John Adams stood before the court and said, "Gentlemen, I am for the prisoners at the bar and shall apologize for it only in the words of the Marquis Beccaria: 'If I can but be the instrument of preserving one life, his blessings and tears shall be sufficient consolation to me for the contempt of mankind!'"

The British soldiers were acquitted, and John Adams recovered the friendship and trust of his fellow citizens. They saw in him what Abigail had seen in the beginning, a man of total integrity.

As a boy, John had been instructed well in religion on Sundays and sermon days. John's father was a man who feared God's justice but loved God as well. As the little boy sat in the plain brown meeting house which was used for a church, he listened to the minister speak often of heaven. What made a great impression was the description of "fields of paradise, everlastingly watered." To young John Adams, sharing a farm boy's concern for the cycles of drought and flood, this seemed marvelous indeed.

When John went to Harvard, he frequently found his religious principles mocked and challenged.

"So you are so sure of God, eh?" some of the other boys would laugh. It annoyed them to see young Adams being so faithful in his religious duties when they had long since forgotten theirs.

"I am very sure of God," the young man would answer. He studied under the brilliant Dr. Winthrop, and one day he was troubled by the charge that there is a basic conflict between science and religion.

"The finest scientists I know are the most devotedly Christian men," Dr. Winthrop assured the young scholar.

When John was about 12 years old, his father told him that sex belonged only in marriage. He said it was a grave sin to take sex without the loving relationship of marriage. When John went to Harvard, many of the boys in his classes would speak of their adventures with various girls. They would laugh about the girls, share stories about them, tell dirty jokes showing what little respect they had for these girls. John was shocked and disgusted. When he began to date Abigail, he resolved that the most beautiful and intimate part of their relationship would be reserved for their married life together.

John and Abigail often went walking in the woods, and John would be delighted by little things about her, such as the way her silky brown hair blew across her face. He would be moved to deep tenderness.

In October of 1764 John Adams married Abigail. After the ceremony she put on a long, scarlet riding cloak and hood, and ran down the steps of her father's house. John lifted her gently onto his horse, and off they sped to the little cottage he had taken. They moved into the house in Boston, and Abigail immediately planted a lilac bush to symbolize how, like the flowers, their deep love for each other would flourish.

In July Abigail was expecting their first baby and unrest was growing in the colonies.

"There are meetings I must attend, but it breaks my heart to leave you, even for a few days," John said.

Abigail smiled, "If it is for freedom, then go."

"You are as fiery as a young grenadier," her young husband laughed, amazed that Abigail was every bit as much a patriot as he.

Abigail and John had five children, one of whom grew up to be president. Each new child was welcomed joyously by the young parents, and one time John almost broke his leg racing home to be there when his child was born, only to walk in upon Abigail busily rocking the newborn and tidying up the house.

Adams served in the Continental Congress, was a negotiator at the Treaty of Paris (which ended the Revolutionary War), became vice president in 1789, and the nation's second president in 1797. When they moved into the largely unfinished presidential residence in Washington, Abigail wrote that none of the rooms were finished and she used the large audience room to dry her clothes. She told her daughter, "You must keep all this to yourself and when asked how I like it, say that I write you the situation is beautiful!"

The Adamses enjoyed 54 years of marriage and loved one another as dearly at the end as they had at the beginning. The genuine affection between them was a source of wonder to outsiders. The religious faith that had united them during their early courtship remained to the end of their lives, and they both continued to see every day as another step on the long journey to heaven.

At midnight, July 3, turned into the dawn of July 4, 1826, John Adams lay dying. It was the 50th anniversary of the founding of the United States. Also dying was another giant from the early days of the Republic, Thomas Jefferson. The nation prayed that both these great men should live to see July 4th and, in fact, at noon of the 4th Jefferson died. In the Adams home, surrounded by his family, the old patriot heard the sounds of saluting cannon and the shouts of "Hooray!" He knew it was the 4th of July and he had lived to see his country's fiftieth anniversary. At sunset on the 4th, John Adams finished the last few steps of that journey to heaven that began in the simple little church in Braintree, Massachusetts. It had been a good journey, undertaken by a noble man.■

FOURTH PRESIDENT 1809-1817

2

Defender of Religious Freedom:
James Madison

James Madison was not a confessed Christian; he was a deist, like many men of his time. He has been included in this anthology of Christian presidents because of his strong stand for religious freedom. Because of his work, and the work of men like him, Christians in this country are free to worship and practice their beliefs openly and freely without fear of persecution.

It was a bright April day in 1777 when the 26-year-old legislator stood to make his speech. Springtime in Virginia was always beautiful, but it seemed this day was even more ideal than usual.

"The young man doesn't have much of a voice," commented a bystander.

"No, but his ideas are good," his companion said. "He speaks about religious freedom. We sure need that. The way things are now, a man can be put in jail for speaking what he believes."

"Madison is a fine young fellow," a well-dressed gentleman said, "from an excellent family. You know, they put some ministers into jail in the next town just for preaching what their consciences told them was truth. That young Madison tried his best to get them released, but he just couldn't do it."

James Madison almost had to shout to be heard. His voice was thin and weak, and his health was very poor. He didn't expect to live much longer, and he told his friends, "I do not expect a long and healthy life. I shall soon be exchanging time for eternity." He said this when he was just 21 years old. He was a small person, 5-foot-6 in height and weighing less than 100 pounds.

"He looks like a little banty rooster," a farmer laughed as the young politician spoke.

"When is he going to pass out the whiskey? That's what I want to know," said a gruff man. It was the custom for all politicians to pass out free whiskey at their speeches. One jug of free whiskey was considered a kind of payment for a man's vote.

Suddenly, James Madison stopped talking and the crowd grew quiet.

"When is the corn liquor coming?" a man shouted.

Madison said sharply, "I do not intend to pass out whiskey. I consider that a corruption of the election process. I have too much respect for you voters to think I might buy you with whiskey!"

There was loud laughter. "He'll never get elected," a red-faced man said. "Who does he think he is? He's no good politican if he doesn't give free whiskey. Why, he ought to be a preacher instead of a politician!"

"Yeah," another man yelled, "go find yourself a pulpit, Madison. We don't need you around here."

The man running against Madison got up then to make his speech. It was a short speech, and then he smiled broadly and said, "Line right up for the free whiskey, boys. Let's all have a good time. And don't you forget who to vote for come election day!"

"That is bribery," cried Madison.

But the election was won by the other man. Madison was so angry that he challenged the results. He argued that it was nothing short of corruption to buy votes with whiskey, but he lost the challenge. There were many political battles ahead, though, that James Madison would win.

Madison was born in Virginia, and even though he considered himself "dull," he had a brilliant mind. He studied Latin at the age of 12, and Hebrew at Princeton University. He seemed at one point destined for the ministry, but he also studied law, and all the while he was doing this he was also teaching his younger brothers and sisters.

Madison studied religion intently and was a diligent student of the Bible. He read every book on theology he could get his hands on, exploring the whole history of Christianity. At a very early age he was deeply offended by the religious intolerance which was common in that part of the country. He became a passionate defender of religious freedom saying, "All men should be free to profess their opinions in matters of religion." He denounced what he called the "diabolical principle of persecution."

Madison's own philosophy of life was summarized in his feelings that "It is the mutual duty of all to practice Christian forbearance, love, and charity towards one another." While he was at Princeton College, there was a religious revival and young James took part in some of the services. When he returned home to his father's house, he sometimes conducted worship services.

In 1778 Madison attended the Constitutional Convention in Philadelphia. His work there was so important that he became know as "the father of the Constitution." Shortly afterwards he was one of the three authors of The Federalist Papers, which explained the Constitution.

In 1794, when Madison was 43, he married a blue-eyed, black-haired Quaker widow named Dorothea (Dolley) Payne Todd. Her first husband had died in a yellow fever outbreak, and the lovely young widow had numerous suitors. She became one of the nation's most popular first ladies, providing a welcome contrast to her quiet and often reserved husband.

In 1809 Madison became president of the United States. During his administration the War of 1812 occurred and

Washington, D.C., was burned by the British army. The president and his wife were forced to flee, and during this harrowing time Dolley earned the affection of the country by saving many valuable national treasures, such as the Stuart painting of George Washington.

After his presidency Madison retired to Montpelier, his estate at the foot of Virginia's Blue Ridge Mountains, and put into effect many excellent ideas on scientific farming. Although there were slaves on his plantation, he personally hated slavery and was always looking for a way to get rid of the institution. Like Washington and Jefferson, Virginia planters who opposed slavery found it hard in their time to act upon their principles.

James Madison never officially joined a church. During his lifetime he was questioned many times on his religious beliefs because some feared that the piety of his youth had been lost in the secular environment of his young adulthood. There is no doubt that Madison always remained a man with a strong faith in God, and the firm conviction that all men are responsible to God for their actions. He said, "Abuse of freedom is an offense against God, and to God, not to man, must an account be rendered."

James Madison always treated religion with respect, never failing to attend public worship in his neighborhood. He frequently invited ministers to his household when family prayers would be conducted. No man so respected the sanctity of religious belief as sacred from the interference of mankind. No man did more to insure it for all Americans.

In the Bill of Rights of Virginia his words stand as a foundation stone for religious freedom in America. The young statesman wrote:

"Religion, or the duty we owe our Creator, and the manner of discharging it, can be directed only by reason and conviction, not by force or violence; and therefore all men are equally entitled to the free exercise of religion according to the dictates of conscience."

In his final years at Montpelier Madison was severely crippled by rheumatism, but he died content with the sure knowledge that because of his efforts Americans had secured the most precious freedom of all—freedom of conscience.■

John Quincy Adams.

SIXTH PRESIDENT 1825-1829

3

A Servant of God: John Quincy Adams

The president of the United States took his seat in the family pew on this special Sunday morning. His heart was deeply moved as he looked around the familiar church and remembered his beloved parents. They had worshiped from this very same pew as for decades they had given him the best of a Christian home. They had been filled to overflowing with the love of God, of each other, and their children.

Tears filled John Quincy Adams' eyes as still another eulogy for his father, John Adams, was being given in this church. John Adams had died a few weeks earlier, and his son was still in deep mourning. The minister's voice filled the silent church as he said, after praising the virtue of John Adams:

"And now, on this special occasion, is there anyone in this church who wishes to express a belief in the divine mission of Christ by rising and coming forth to pledge to live according to the Gospel?"

John Quincy Adams stood and came forward. He had become a professed Christian in public. Before becoming president, John never officially joined a church, though he had deep religious beliefs. He attended services as a child at the Congregational church in Braintree, and he started each day of his life by reading a chapter or two from the Bible, but he was not officially a member of a church until he came forth this day.

Adams always believed strongly in obedience to the will of God, and he saw public worship as a Christian obligation and family duty.

The eldest son of President John Adams, and the only son of a president to himself attain that high office, John had a fortunate childhood. His greatest blessing was the love of his devoted parents, but he also had the advantages of world travel. At the age of 10 he went to France with his father, and he lived for a while in Moscow while his father served in the diplomatic corps.

Throughout his public life Adams had unshakable integrity, and this often made him the subject of bitter attacks. He lived by the quote, "The magistrate is the servant, not of his own desires, not even of the people, but of his God." When he was elected to Congress in 1803, Adams strictly followed his Puritan conscience even when it meant alienating his political allies, as it often did.

One of the causes dear to the heart of Adams was the plight of the American Indian. He demanded that Congress provide land for the displaced Indians to live in peace and safety. Very few congressmen at this, or any other, time were concerned about the Indians because they were so few in number that they had no real political influence.

John Adams, the congressman's father, had written to Thomas Jefferson: "I have felt a compassion for the Indians since my childhood. There was one family in my town whose wigwam was within a mile of my house. This family was frequently at my father's house and I, in my boyish rambles, used to call at their wigwam, where I never failed to be treated with whortle berries, blackberries, strawberries, or apples." The father often told John Quincy Adams of these experiences, giving the younger man a lifelong affection for the Indians. He never ceased trying to improve their welfare.

John Quincy Adams also opposed slavery and was so determined an abolitionist that he earned the name "the madman from Massachusetts" from pro-slavery forces.

As he always tried to be the "servant of God," Adams was called a "Lucifer" by the Federalists, a party scavenger, a popularity seeker, and a renegade. Still, he held sternly to his principles and, while being deserted by all his friends, said, "I can never be sufficiently grateful to Providence that my father and my mother didn't desert me."

At age 30 John married the gentle, graceful Louisa Johnson, and they were as devoted a couple as his parents were. Even while stationed in the bitter cold of Russia while Adams served as U.S. minister there, the couple cheerfully endured the hardships.

In 1825 Adams became president of the United States, but during his term in office his policy of placing principle above party continued to make enemies. He was not elected to a second term, but he returned to the House of Representatives, where he earned the name "old man eloquent."

Throughout his life Adams spent much time in meditation and Bible reading. He saw his attendance at church as providing tremendous strength in his life. He wrote: "Hope in the goodness of God, reliance upon His mercy in affliction, trust in Him to bring light out of darkness and good out of evil, are the comforts and promises which I desire from public worship. They help to sustain me in the troubles that are thickening upon me. . . ."

Adams saw immortal life as a blessed continuation of man's existence here on earth. Above all, he looked to the example of Jesus Christ to guide his conduct. Every night, before he went to sleep, no matter if he was in Massachusetts or Russia, no matter who was present, he said aloud the prayer his mother had taught him as a child:

Now I lay me down to sleep,
I pray the Lord my soul to keep;
If I should die before I wake,
I pray the Lord my soul to take.

Adams did not mumble the words either. He said them clearly and loudly, a fact verified by a friend, Dr. George Ellis, who shared a hotel room with him in 1844.

The words that gave Adams comfort during his life appear often in his diaries and letters. They are words like Almighty God, Disposer of events, Job, Psalms, truth and conscience. The things he found repugnant were treachery, slander, idleness, and bitterness. He refused ever to lower his standards for the approval of the world.

When the Mexican War was fought and a large land area annexed to the United States, the conflict was very popular. On Feb. 21, 1848, the House of Representatives was alive with patriotic excitement. Swords of honor were being given to the generals who won the war.

One by one the soldiers, their chests ablaze with medals, stepped into the seats reserved for them. As each officer appeared, the congressmen stood up to clap and shout ringing hurrahs.

Suddenly, a frail and bent figure arose from his place in the Massachusetts delegation.

"It's Adams," a younger congressman noted with annoyance. "Chances are he is going to make trouble, as he usually does."

The 81-year-old former president cleared his throat and began, in a surprisingly strong voice, to point out the injustices involved in the Mexican War.

"Doesn't the old man realize everybody disagrees with him?" a southern congressman snapped.

A New England legislator who knew Adams well smiled and said, "Ah yes, but has it ever mattered to Adams what public opinion is?"

A few moments later John Quincy Adams staggered and collapsed in his chair. He had suffered a heart attack, and in two days he was dead.

Only now would the entire nation realize what a man of principle John Quincy Adams was. His political foe Martin Van Buren said of him, "He was an honest man, not only incorruptible himself, but an enemy to corruption everywhere." Theodore

Parker, a well-known theologian and reformer, said, "The slave has lost a champion, America has lost a man who loved her with his whole heart, religion has lost a supporter, and freedom has lost an unfailing friend."

John Quincy Adams was given a final salute by the minute guns on top of Penn's Hill, where he had stood as a boy with his mother and watched the Battle of Bunker Hill across the Back Bay. As those who loved Adams wept, the pastor of his church, William Lunt, preached from Revelation:

"Be thou faithful unto death, and I will give thee a crown of life." ■

EIGHTH PRESIDENT 1837-1841

4

Defender of the Poor: Martin Van Buren

The handsome little blond boy appeared a little past dawn at the law office. He wore the coarse linen and rough woolens his mother had spun and woven for him.

"Ah," the tall man looked down at the boy, "you must be Mat. Do you know what your duties are to be, lad?"

The small boy nodded, "I am to sweep out the office and dust the furniture."

"Yes," the man said, "and also it is your job to keep the logs blazing in the fireplace on cold days. If you do well at all these tasks, then you shall be a law clerk. You will go with me to the court and copy for me and carry my bag. And when my regular law clerk is away, you shall sleep here all night and guard the place. Do you understand all of that?"

"Yes, sir," said 13-year-old Martin Van Buren. He was no stranger to hard work. As a young boy he had worked in his father's tavern, mopping the floors, straightening the tables. In the winter, when it was bitter cold, he would carry in the logs and keep the tavern warm. While the very small children waited for good <u>Sint Nikolaas</u> to bring nuts from Muscat, apples from Orange, and plums from Spain, Martin would be doing a man's work.

Now, the boy was excited to be working in a real law office. A serious boy, he wanted to someday be a lawyer himself, but he never attended legal school. He would sometimes go to the taverns where court cases were conducted and would watch with awe as the lawyers shouted at each other. He dreamed of being one of those lawyers himself.

Young Mat performed his duties well at the law office. It wasn't long before he was finishing up all his duties and then coming to court to do copy work.

Often, during a trial, whiskey would be freely passed around until nearly everybody in the court was drunk. In those days watching a trial was frequently the chief source of entertainment. If the spectators didn't like a verdict, they would sometimes attack the lawyers and the jury.

One day Mat was copying in the courtroom when suddenly the lawyer he worked for turned to him. "How old are you now, Mat?"

"Fifteen," the boy said.

"Have you been listening well to this case, lad?"

"Yes, sir," Mat said.

"Then here, you sum up the case."

The boy could hardly believe his ears. He was being asked to sum up a court case, to give the final argument to the jury! His heart raced with excitement. He was very short for his age, so he had to climb on top of a chair so he could be seen while he was talking. He began to speak in a low, nervous voice, but soon he gained confidence. His voice grew louder, and he was putting some emotion into his words. The courtroom became very silent as everybody stared at the blond lad who was summing up a real court case.

The old lawyer smiled at his young law clerk. He gave Mat a

silver half dollar and said, "Now you are a lawyer."

The boy almost burst with pride.

Martin Van Buren was born in December of 1782 in Kinderhook, New York. Ten days later he was baptized in the Dutch Reformed Church where his uncle was a deacon. The little boy was a welcome Christmas blessing to his parents, who already had two little girls and very much wanted a son.

Christmas was always a joyful occasion in Kinderhook, but this year it was best of all in the Van Buren household. The Revolutionary War had ended, the Van Burens had a new infant son, and economic prosperity was all around.

The child was raised strictly by loving, dutiful parents, and the faith he received in Kinderhook became a sturdy support throughout his life. As an adult he could always be found on Sundays at the local church singing hymns in his loud voice. In his old age he was a familiar sight in his high-backed pew at the little Dutch church; he wore bearskin gloves during the winter, and inside the church he would place one of the gloves atop his head to keep warm. When he stood to join in the singing, he would hold tight to the furry glove to keep it in place. The church was crowded with people, but during the singing the voice of Martin Van Buren could be heard joyously praising God above everyone else's voice.

As a young lawyer Van Buren frequently used his profession in defense of the poor. He had a particular hatred for the widespread cruelty of debtors prison. Men who were behind in their debts were thrown into prison with hardened criminals, ruining their lives and the lives of their families.

In those years every poor person lived in constant dread of debtors prison. The most honest man could end up in the prison if he suffered some crop failure or a horse went lame, or if for any reason he couldn't pay his bills.

In March of 1813 young Van Buren sat on the Court for the Correction of Errors, which was the highest court in New York. Before the court came the case of a poor man who had allegedly escaped from debtors prison and was therefore being severely punished.

The case was tragic and unusual. A new law had just been passed allowing men imprisoned in debtors prison to leave the jail for brief periods of freedom, during which time they could visit their families or try to get some work to save their families from starvation. The men had to stay within a few miles of the prison, and if they strayed beyond these limits they were considered escaped criminals.

In this case the poor man was a farmer and he had used his freedom to put his only cow out to pasture. The cow wandered about 10 feet beyond the limits of the man's legal area and when he crossed over the line to recover the cow, he was arrested as an escapee. His creditor, the man he owed the money to, had been watching him and called the sheriff. The poor man took his case to a higher court when he received a harsh sentence for prison escape.

Van Buren stood up in the court and spoke with intense emotion. His voice rang out like a clear bell. He bitterly condemned the whole system of debtors prison, saying: "It forces men from society and from their friends and their agonized families, into the dreary walls of a prison, not for crimes which they have committed; not for frauds which they have practiced, but for the misfortune of being poor."

Van Buren's voice blazed on, accusing the debtors prison of erasing the difference between guilt and innocence, of allowing greedy creditors to act like ravenous wolves devouring the poor. His eloquence caused the decision against the poor farmer to be reversed. The young Dutch lawyer here demonstrated what was characteristic of his life—a deep affection for humanity, especially for the most downtrodden of people. His Christianity was not confined to the walls of a church but was carried out in the deeds of mercy he practiced in his daily life.

During Van Buren's life he had many nicknames, including "the little magician," which paid tribute to his political skill. President Andrew Jackson said of him, "It is said he is a great magician. I believe it, but his only wand is good common sense which he uses for the benefit of his country."

Speaking of his nicknames, one version of the origin of the expression, "OK" is that is stood for "Old Kinderhook," a reference to Van Buren.

At the age of 24 Van Buren married his childhood sweetheart, Hannah Hoes, and they had four sons. He rose quickly in politics, moving from U.S. senator in 1821 to governor of New York in 1828 and vice president in 1832. In 1836 he was elected president, but his administration was not a happy one because a severe economic recession hit the country. Defeated after one term, Van Buren took it in good humor. One friend described him as "immovable, stubborn, and good natured through everything."

Van Buren's political career did not end with his loss of the presidency. In 1848 he joined a faction of the Democratic party that was bitterly opposed to slavery. They were called Barnburners because they were compared to a farmer trying to burn down the barn to rid himself of rats. Enemies charged they were burning down the Democratic party over the issue of slavery. It was no wonder, though, that the kindhearted man from Kinderhook could not stand slavery any more than he could stand the brutality of seeing innocent men in debtors prison. Van Buren failed to be elected to office again, and he retired to private life.

During the last years of his life Van Buren and one of his sons took a two-year trip through Europe. It was probably the happiest time of his life, and everywhere he went he received a warm welcome.

When the old man returned to his farm in New York, he learned that the entire village of Kinderhook was celebrating his birthday. He was 72 and a beloved figure in the little town. In the summer he would ride to church in his famous English coach, and in the winter he would ride in his high-fronted sleigh, brass bells jingling.

When Van Buren died, he was buried beside the woman he had dearly loved all his life, Hannah. He wanted no ringing of bells and no music except for the hymn that had been his favorite all his life, "O God, Our Help in Ages Past." Two ministers who were good friends of the family conducted the funeral service, and the Stars and Stripes were draped over the altar during the ceremony. The pew that Martin Van Buren had unfailingly occupied during life was draped in black. Red shirted members of the Kinderhook Fire Engine Company led the procession to the cemetery, and cannon thundered throughout the countryside in final tribute to the president.

The blond Dutch boy who had won numerous legal cases while still a teenager, born of common, hard-working, and ill-educated people, had carried throughout his life integrity, sincerity, and devotion to his obligations. At his baptism, on a chill day in December, his godmother had promised to see that he was brought up in the faith of his fathers. He had been. What is more, he had put that faith into practice, fulfilling the Biblical command to be not only hearers of the Word but also doers of it.■

John Tyler

TENTH PRESIDENT 1841-1845

5

The Rebel President: John Tyler

Court came to order in Charles City, and the bystanders glanced at the wretched-looking prisoner. He had been accused of injuring a man in a tavern brawl. He had a bad reputation before the incident, and there was little doubt that he would be convicted and sent to prison for a long time.

"Who is the poor fool's lawyer?" a young man asked his companion.

"None other than John Tyler," the companion said wryly, "who must be a fool himself to take such a hopeless case."

The other man seemed surprised. "Why, that's Judge Tyler's son from Greenway Plantation. He cannot have the good sense of his father, to be involved in such a matter."

John Tyler was 21 years old, with a prominent thin Roman nose, silky brown hair, bright blue eyes, a warm smile, and a silvery voice. He had been educated at William and Mary College and was already a member of the Virginia House of Delegates. Now, he stepped up to the jury and began to speak in defense of the accused.

Tyler explained the background of the prisoner, how he had never had the advantages of good Christian parents, a decent education, a happy childhood.

The murmuring in the courtroom died down. Suddenly there was total silence. The young lawyer spoke effectively, making good use of all his emotional arguments. He explained how the man stole in the past because he was driven by desperate need. Tyler admitted the man had been drinking and brawling, but he pleaded eloquently that the jury place itself in this poor man's shoes. Having a sorry life like this, wouldn't they also be tempted to turn to drink?

"He's quite an orator," a spectator said, "and perhaps not so much the fool as people are saying."

Young John Tyler frequently took criminal cases that no other lawyer would touch. Using his brilliant eloquence and his charm, he often won sympathy for accused men, securing for them another chance in life when they were all but certain to go to prison. Tyler's remarkable success in the courtroom brought him to the attention of all of Virginia. Eventually he was being compared with such orators as Daniel Webster, Henry Clay, and John Calhoun.

Born in Virginia in 1790, John lost his mother at age seven. His upbringing became the total responsibility of Judge Tyler, his father, a stern but kindly man with a strong belief in states rights. The little boy was often frail and sickly, but he was extremely bright. He had a gentle character, which he inherited from his mother, and sometimes his father feared he wouldn't be tough enough to handle himself in the world.

An incident that occurred when John was only 10 years old proved to the Judge that underneath the boy's gentle manners was a steel personality. John attended a school run by a Scotchman named McMurdo, who regularly whipped his students. Tyler commented in later years that it was a wonder McMurdo hadn't beaten the brains out of every scholar he taught. One day young

42

Tyler led a revolt against McMurdo. When the outraged school-master went to Judge Tyler to demand that the boy be punished, the Judge sternly said, "Sic semper tyrannis," the motto of Virginia, which means, "Thus may it ever be to tyrants!"

John was raised with strong religious convictions, and as a young man, as well as throughout his life, he was troubled by the existence of slavery. His father owned slaves, as did Tyler himself. Young Tyler did fight the continuation of the African slave trade and campaigned for laws that banned the buying and selling of slaves in Washington, D.C. He saw black people being sold in the nation's capital, and the sight made him physically sick. Like many men of goodwill in the Virginia tidewater region, he hoped that the slave population could slowly be sent into the territories to start new lives, no further slaves would be imported, and the institution of slavery would gradually die out. Sadly, this would prove a vain hope.

At the age of 23 Tyler married Letitia Christian, a sweet and beautiful girl. In a note, he wrote to her: "To ensure you happiness is now my only object, and whether I float or sink in the stream of fortune, you may be assured of this, that I shall never cease to love you." Seven children were born to the couple and lovingly raised by the devoutly religious Letitia. She was unselfish and totally devoted to her family. In her late 40s she suffered a stroke and remained an invalid until her death at the age of 52.

John Tyler was a congressman, the governor of Virginia, and a U.S. senator. Then, in 1836, he left the Democratic party and became a Whig, joining William Henry Harrison on the ticket in 1840. The "Tippecanoe and Tyler Too" campaign put Harrison in the White House and, after only one month, when Harrison died, made John Tyler the first vice president in American history to succeed to the presidency through the death of the president. Tyler, by bold and decisive action, set a precedent by which all succeeding vice presidents considered themselves presidents with full powers upon taking office. At 51 Tyler also became the youngest man ever to serve as president.

After Letitia's death, Tyler's daughter acted as first lady until the last few months of his term when he married Julia Gardiner. After he left the White House, he and Julie retired to his Sherwood Forest plantation. A bright and vivacious girl, Julia was also a devoted Christian. She bore Tyler another seven children, and he lavished upon these new little ones, the same loving attention he gave to the children of his first marriage. He would bounce them joyfully on his knee and watch their progress with warm concern. When President Tyler and Julia were married at the Church of the Ascension, it was the first time a president had been married while in office.

The religious faith of John Tyler, acquired as a boy, deepened as he grew older. Reverence was always an important part of his character, and as president he worshiped at St. John's Episcopal Church. He always expressed a firm belief in God and in the value of solitude and suffering as an aid to spiritual growth. He meditated often at Sherwood Forest, and during the onslaught of illness and pain and sorrow he often spoke of the encouragement he received from reading the Bible and deepening his Christian faith. He felt that all suffering had a purpose. Once, after a very severe illness, he said, "Nothing but the kind providence of our heavenly Father could have saved me." He spoke frequently to his pastor and once described experiencing Christ in a very personal way. He said that his life had always been illuminated by a "bright faith in the Christian religion."

Sherwood Forest was a model plantation, using the latest scientific methods. There were slaves, but they were treated in a humanitarian manner and there was none of the brutality of whip and chain found at some other plantations. Still, it was slavery, and it was a thorn in Tyler's conscience. During the 1850s, as the nation hurtled towards the bloody Civil War, Tyler kept on preaching moderation, hoping for a peaceful solution to the terrible dilemma of slavery. In 1861, however, when Virginia seceded from the Union, the former president made the same bitter decision as his fellow Virginian Robert E. Lee. He cast his lot with the Confederacy, fighting to defend an institution, slavery, which he did not even favor.

44

Now over 70, and beset with serious illness, Tyler was elected to the Confederate Congress. The tragic reality of a former president now denounced as a rebel by the country he had led was a terrible sorrow to Tyler's final years. In debt and branded as a traitor, the former president was stricken ill on Jan. 12, 1862. He died with a peaceful smile on his face two days later, consoled by the only thing that had remained constant in his troubled life, his Christian faith.

In eulogy, Tyler was described as "an honest, affectionate, benevolent, loving man." He was buried from St. Paul's Episcopal Church and taken to a knoll overlooking his beloved James River, where he was entombed beside President James Monroe. His final years were part of the agony of the nation at large, where families and friends were torn apart in loyalties.

After Tyler's death, Union soldiers came to Sherwood Forest and sacked and plundered the beautiful old plantation. One young soldier found, amidst the debris and ashes, a book.

"What's this?" he brashly said. "Think it belonged to the old rebel himself? Maybe this is where he wrote down the latest prices of corn and wheat. Understand he made fat profits. . . ." But then the soldier shook the dust and ashes from the book and found it wasn't a book of accounts after all. It was John Tyler's Bible, the holy book he opened often to find consolation.

The grin left the boy's face. The blue-clad soldier gently brushed the book clean.

John Tyler's Bible was given to his widow, who years later gave it to the president's son. Like John Tyler, the book had seen the sorrow and the fire. In a way it was symbolic of the man who owned it.■

James Buchanan

FIFTEENTH PRESIDENT 1857-1861

6

The Good Uncle: James Buchanan

Dr. John King was pastor of the little church in Mercersburg, Pennsylvania. He was an amazing man, a great scholar and also a man so fully a Christian in his life that people could not help but admire him. He preached to the hardworking pioneer folk in the settlements around his church, and he spoke simply but eloquently about what it means to follow Christ. He provided the most stirring sermon in the way his own life was conducted. He truly practiced what he preached.

One of the families sitting on a rough-hewn pew in front were the Buchanans of Cove Gap. There were 10 children in the family, and one of them was a sturdy little boy named James. He looked up at the minister and was deeply impressed. Years later, when he was himself a man, he would say he had never known a human being for whom he felt a greater reverence. For all of James Buchanan's life he would never forget Dr. King and the kindly Christian spirit he demonstrated.

James Buchanan's father was a stern man who spent most of his time thinking about making money. He loved James, but he was never quite satisfied with the boy's efforts, no matter how hard he worked. The elder Buchanan wanted perfection, so he always left his son with the uneasy feeling that he wasn't quite measuring up. The boy's mother was totally different from the father, and she provided a gentler influence in James' life. She was a deeply religious Christian with a strong but simple philosophy—follow the Ten Commandments and the Sermon on the Mount and accept whatever happens as God's will.

The elder Buchanan wanted his son to become a financial success as early in life as possible, so he sent him to college at age 16. The father was haunted by the fear that he might die and leave his wife and children destitute, so he wanted to be sure young James could take over the family responsibilities. James worked hard at school and opened a law office which was an immediate success.

In the midst of Buchanan's successful law practice, a personal tragedy struck his life which was to have a lifelong impact. The handsome young lawyer was introduced to a slim, beautiful, dark-haired girl named Ann Caroline Coleman. Almost the moment that James looked into her shining dark eyes, he fell in love with her. Unfortunately, the girl's father was a wealthy, suspicious man who feared all his daughter's suitors were fortune hunters. He wanted his daughter to marry a man of equal social status and wealth; he had already married his eldest daughter off to a prominent judge. Although the Buchanan family was now quite successful in business, they were a far cry from the Colemans, with mansions all over Pennsylvania and tables ever heavy with fine foods, wines, and brandy. At first the social difference did not bother Ann, who dearly loved the good-looking, 6-foot-tall lawyer who courted her, but it deeply troubled her parents.

The young couple became engaged in 1819, but then James was called away on political business. He was growing more active in the Democratic party and was serving in the state legislature. In his absence Ann's parents convinced her that if the young man

48

really loved her, nothing could induce him to leave her side. The proud, impulsive, and self-willed girl angrily wrote a note to James accusing him of not loving her sufficiently and being more interested in her father's money than her. James was deeply hurt. Later there was unfounded gossip about James and a neighbor girl, further enraging Ann. In a burst of anger she broke off the engagement.

The final act in the tragedy was played out when, on Dec. 9, Ann Coleman became mysteriously ill and died at her sister's home. The doctor said she was suffering from hysterical convulsions. Crushed by grief, James Buchanan pleaded with Ann's father to be allowed to see her body and to walk as a mourner in her funeral. He wrote to the father:

"It is now no time for explanation, but the time will come when you will discover that she, as well as I, have been much abused. God forgive the authors of it. I may sustain the shock of her death, but I feel that happiness has fled from me forever."

The note was returned by the Colemans unopened, and Buchanan was not permitted to attend the funeral. James Buchanan was so deeply crushed by the death of his fiancee that it was difficult for him to ever form another friendship with a girl. He remained unmarried, becoming the only bachelor in the U.S. presidency.

Buchanan returned to his family for comfort, and his mother proved a great support. Once again she told him of her own strong belief that everything that happens, even misfortune, happens for a purpose and that only God knows the ultimate value of it.

In 1820 Buchanan was elected to the House of Representatives, and later he was elected to the Senate. During these years early death by tuberculosis dogged his brothers and sisters, and he was forced to take charge of his orphaned nieces and nephews. To these he gave the love and affection that would have gone to his children had he married.

Buchanan's sister Sarah died at 27, leaving a little daughter, Elizabeth. His sister Harriet was widowed young and left with a 5-year-old boy, James Buchanan Henry. Harriet was herself ill with tuberculosis, and James wrote to her: "You are welcome, most welcome, to a home with me, where I think you may promote my happiness as well as your own."

Another sister, Jane, was dying, leaving three young children behind. Buchanan's sister Maria struggled with economic hardship and a desperate effort to move her child, Jessie, to a better climate which would be more favorable to her ailing lungs. Little Jessie was her uncle's favorite, and he was determined to send her to the very best country school. Jessie was not brilliant, but she was a sweet child. Buchanan said, "If not very smart, she is very good, and that is better."

Buchanan felt a deep, lifelong responsibility for all these children. He lamented that tuberculosis would soon cause him to have an entire orphanage of children to worry about. As the only financially successful member of the family, everyone depended on him for help in any emergency. Buchanan tried not to make his relatives dependent on him, and he hoped he could somehow help them while letting them retain their self-respect.

Although he saw slavery as a great moral evil, Buchanan hoped the issue could be resolved without war. Because he favored moderation, he became the Democratic choice for president in 1856. Deeply committed to the preservation of the Union, Buchanan tried to hold back the rising passions threatening the peace, but reason was not to prevail. When in 1861 Abraham Lincoln came to office, the war had already begun and James Buchanan went sadly into private life.

Prior to leaving the White House, Buchanan went to New York and had a serious talk about religion with Rev. William Paxton. He talked about the meaning of regeneration, atonement, repentance, and faith, and in the end he said to the minister, "Well, sir, I hope I am a Christian. I think I have much of the experience which you describe, and as soon as I retire I will unite with the Presbyterian Church."

Rev. Paxton asked, "Why delay in joining the church until after you leave the presidency?"

"I must delay for the honor of religion," the President said. He

50

feared that some might consider his move a political one rather than a religious act and it would be considered hypocritical.

In retirement Buchanan continued to care for his many poor and ailing relatives with true Christian charity. On Sept. 23, 1865, convinced of his sincere piety, the elders of his church admitted him to Communion. In May of 1868 Buchanan fell seriously ill, and he gave instructions that when he died there were to be no great tributes or pomp-gilded ceremonies. He wanted his funeral to be as simply as his life had been. Arrogance was never one of Buchanan's faults. Once, when he was president, he was visited by the Prince of Wales, who brought such a large party with him that there wasn't room for all the dignitaries. The president promptly gave up his own bedroom and slept on the couch.

The day before Buchanan died he said, "I have always felt and still feel that I discharged every public duty imposed on me conscientiously."

Monday morning, June 1, 1868, Buchanan died. Contrary to his wishes, thousands came to pay him a final tribute. His friends remembered him as a man of integrity, charity, kindness, and courtesy. In his will he left generous gifts to his chruch, and to the city of Lancaster to be given to the poor for fuel in the wintertime. One of the cruelest deprivations suffered by the Lancaster poor was the bitter cold of winter without the money to buy fuel. Buchanan also provided for his servants and his large family.

To the nation James Buchanan left the memory of a man who always remained common and familiar, with gracious manners and unfailing gentleness. In his relations with his barber and his gardener he acted no differently than he did with heads of state. He was always a Christian gentleman, never dishonoring the philosophy impressed upon him while a small boy listening to his Mercersburg pastor.■

James A. Garfield.

TWENTIETH PRESIDENT 1881

7

The Preacher President: James Garfield

The handsome young evangelist stood to his full 6-foot height as small crowds collected at the lake. Feathery clouds sailed like clipper ships across the night sky, and a steady murmur of voices blended with the evening wind. The young man had preached in other small towns, but these people had never seen him before. They studied him carefully, the muscular lad with thick brown hair and lively blue eyes who looked more like a merchant seaman than a man of God.

"I hear he's good," a woman remarked. "I've been told he sometimes preaches in German and English."

"What's his regular work?" her husband demanded. "Will you look at the callouses on his hands? I'd say he's worked more with those stout arms than with his speech."

"Well," commented a young girl, "nothing wrong with a Christian man being a hardworking fellow. Jesus was a carpenter."

A hush fell as the young man began to speak. "I've come tonight to speak with this poor tongue about Jesus. I've come to ask you to do what I did when I was 18 years old, to choose the undying Jesus as your friend and helper, because the hopes of the world are false and the Christian never dies."

His fine voice seemed to roll like thunder across the green hills, up to heaven itself.

"He transports a body to heaven with his very voice," a woman said.

He spoke on, and there was nothing in the night but his voice—solemn, gentle, sometimes soft, and sometimes like an organ in a mighty cathedral. When he finished, a young man arose to come forward and give his life to Jesus. Soon another man came forward, then a woman, then a thin stream of people, and finally a river of people.

It was the 30th time that James Abram Garfield had preached that year, and it had been the same every place he went. He had a way of inspiring his listeners to come forward and accept Jesus. He was such a fine preacher that his mother took it for granted that he would devote his life to the ministry. But the young man was destined to serve his God and his people in other ways.

During his youth Garfield taught school. He was noted for a fatherly attitude towards his students, never being too busy to help a homesick boy over a rough spot. At other times, when a tough student would challenge Garfield, he was equal to it. One time a boy was angry at being corrected and he waited for the young teacher outside the classroom with a stick. His aim was to administer a beating to the teacher, who was only a few years older than himself. Garfield engaged in a rough and tumble scrap that convinced the student that he was indeed master of his classroom.

During the Civil War Garfield formed a company of young volunteers in the Union Army. He led his men with great courage and skill, but here, as in all aspects of his life, his deep Christian beliefs permeated his thinking. In a bitter-cold drizzling rain at the Battle of Middle Creek, the young Union officer came upon the dead bodies of 10 Confederate boys. He said, "Something went out of me that never came back." He spoke sadly of the sacredness of life and the bitter contradictions of war. Throughout his army life, bitterness against the foe was never a part of his thought. Once he was speaking in a small town and some Southern sympathizers began to heckle him and throw eggs at him. He said he had just come from fighting valiant rebel boys whom he respected and he hated to see their memory desecrated by cowardly hecklers. The crowd fell instantly silent.

James Garfield married a devoted Christian woman named Lucretia, and the deep love between Jim and Crete lasted throughout their lives. In the letters Garfield sent home when he was away from his family, his love for them and his Christianity are constantly reemphasized. The first daughter of the family was nicknamed "Trot," and she was dearly loved by both her parents. From a battlefield near Corinth, Mississippi, Garfield wrote to his wife, "Kiss our precious little Trot for me a hundred times. God bless you and her with the richest of His infinite love." When lung fever claimed the life of the beloved child at the age of three, her father was consoled by his strong belief in eternal life.

Garfield was always involved in the spiritual education of his children, sending his son Harry to a private religious school when he felt a secular education was a danger to the boy. He would take long walks in the woods with his children and hand-made the cradle for his younger sons. One time his small boy, Jimmy, told his father he believed in Jesus—but what proofs of his religion could he tell his skeptical classmates? Garfield sat on the steps of the family house and had a long talk with Jimmy, eventually giving the boy's faith the support it needed.

As a very young man Garfield debated a well-known antireligious speaker named John Denton. Denton had been traveling around Ohio and the Northeast in 1858 with great success, usually debating far less skilled men than himself and winning many over to his views. The 26-year-old Garfield arrived at the lecture hall well prepared, and this man who was many years the evangelist's senior found himself astounded. Denton had sought to prove that scientific fact and religious truth were in hopeless conflict, but on every point young Garfield proved as well versed in science as he was in religion, and he was the first person to win a debate over Denton.

When Garfield chose a career in politics, it was not before much soul searching. He had always believed that politics was too dirty a business for a Christian man to participate in. Slowly though, he began to wonder if government couldn't be a Christian vocation after all. He decided that he could help people in government as he had done in teaching and, indeed, when he became an officeholder, he was always sympathetic to the problems of the least important constituents.

Garfield's time in politics was not free from accusation and scandal, though he strove to hew close to his own high ideals. At a time in U.S. history when corruption was rampant, he remained a man of modest means, struggling with the costs of a growing family, even extending his poor resources to help his destitute sister and her family. Garfield's diary, which he kept all his life, is full of instances where, as a high elected official, he would still go great distances to save a few dollars on the family food budget. When other politicians were reaping handsome financial rewards, he found it necessary to pinch his pennies to stretch the family income.

It was almost by accident that James Abram Garfield became president. Chosen as the candidate of a deadlocked Republican convention, he won the presidency in 1880. After only a few months in office, he was shot by a demented assassin.

James Garfield suffered through his painful last illness with the same Christian forbearance that had characterized his life. He died with the grace with which he lived. Though not yet 50 and in the peak of vigor, Garfield was shot at 20 minutes past nine on July 2, 1881, as he stood in the railroad station in Washington. He still had young children, and a great task in government to perform—his dream of reforming Civil Service. One bullet struck him in the back and, remarkably, he remained fully conscious as he was carried from the station. Although the bullet had torn his spinal column and he was in great pain, all the bystanders who watched with sadness and horror remarked about his "steadiness of soul."

When Garfield was told of his grave condition, he said simply, "I can bear it. I am prepared to die." Hope continued, though there was internal bleeding and the president's apparent state of collapse caused his family near despair.

Until Sept. 19, nearly three months after being shot, Garfield lived in great pain and with unfailing courage. The entire nation was profoundly moved by his Christian fortitude, and grieved his death.

At James Garfield's funeral the eulogy was delivered by James Blaine. He concluded by saying: "We believe that in the silence of the receding world he (Garfield) heard the great waves breaking on a farther shore and felt already on his wasted brow the breadth of the eternal morning."

Nothing so befitted the untimely passing of this good and generous man, this Christian gentleman, as his old friend being final witness to the faith that was the hallmark of James Garfield's life. ■

TWENTY-FIRST PRESIDENT 1881-1885

8

The Case of Elizabeth Jennings:

Chester Arthur

Elizabeth Jennings climbed aboard the streetcar on a warm day in mid-July 1854. She was pleased to find a vacant seat in the middle of the car, and she wearily settled down for the journey home. She was a public school teacher and the day had been particularly trying. It was so hot in the classroom, and the children, packed in as they were in their little desks, were very restless. It felt good now to sit down at last after rushing around the schoolroom checking arithmetic and spelling tests.

Elizabeth opened her bag and took out some tests she had yet to grade. She began reading when the harsh voice of a man startled her. She had been so busy with her spelling tests that she hadn't noticed the train stop and the conductor angrily coming towards her.

"Just who do you think you are?" the conductor shouted.

Elizabeth looked up, speechless.

The conductor sneered, "You know very well what I mean, Missy. Don't you act smart like you don't know what I'm talking about. This car is reserved for white folks, and you know it. I want no trouble with pushy colored people like you, so you just get up and go where your kind belongs!"

Elizabeth was frightened, but she was angry too. She was a public school teacher in New York City, and she thought it was her right to sit anywhere she wanted. "I paid for this seat and I intend to sit right here until my street comes up," she said in a firm voice, although her knees were weak.

The conductor reached for the teacher's arm and pulled her to her feet. The spelling tests flew all over the floor. "You want me to throw you off this train, Missy?"

Elizabeth picked up her spelling tests. The conductor was stronger than she was, and he was obviously a brute. There was nothing to do but get off the Third Avenue car. As Elizabeth moved down the aisle, the conductor gave her a rough shove. "You get moving and stay in your place after this!"

Elizabeth's heart was pounding with rage. That night the black people of her neighborhood got together to figure out a plan. Elizabeth Jennings was a respectable professional woman. Nobody had the right to shove her around just because she was black.

"I think we should hire a lawyer and take the case to court," Elizabeth said.

A man laughed. "What lawyer would take the case? You have more faith in the courts than I do. If you ask me, Elizabeth, there is nothing black people like us can do but just get steaming mad."

"I teach my children in school that America is a place with justice for all," Elizabeth insisted. "I intend to find a lawyer and fight this!"

So the next day Elizabeth Jennings found herself sitting across a desk from a 24-year-old attorney named Chester Arthur. He was six-foot-two, and his friends described him as "slender as a maypole." He had dark brown hair and bright black eyes, and he was strikingly handsome. In a clear, determined voice Elizabeth explained how she had been manhandled by the conductor and ordered from her seat just because she was black.

"We will take the case," said the young lawyer, "and we will win it!"

Chester Arthur went into court and argued that the Third Avenue Railroad Company had unfairly violated the rights of Elizabeth Jennings, a woman of good character.

The jury argued among themselves for a while, and then they came up with a verdict. Chester Arthur and Elizabeth Jennings had won.

"It is the order of this court," said the judge, "that the railroad company pay $250 in damages to this lady for the indignity that she suffered on this unhappy occasion."

The case proved to be a landmark. All railroad companies in New York integrated their cars, and never again was a black person there subjected to what had happened to the schoolteacher on that hot July day.

It was not the first time young Arthur had argued a case involving the rights of black Americans. Earlier he had taken part in the Lemmon slave case, where eight Virginia slaves were being taken through New York by their master. The slaves argued that since they were temporarily residing in a free state, they ought to get their freedom. They won freedom, much to the anger of the Virginia political authorities.

Like his father, a Baptist minister, Arthur was an abolitionist. In a trip through Kansas in 1857 he had the chance to see the bitter issue of slavery boiling over into violence. Chester Arthur attended a Republican political meeting in Leavenworth, and he had to take cover when pro- and anti-slavers began shooting it out. Later, while riding in the Kansas countryside, his companion tossed him a pistol with the curt remark, "You might have to use this, Chet. The pro-slavery men know where we stand, and they just might want to shoot our heads off!" No sooner had the man spoken but what two tough-looking men came riding out of the brush, saw that Arthur and his companion were armed, and galloped off.

Chester Arthur was born in 1830 in Fairfield, Vermont, the

child of deeply religious parents. It was a sorrow to the parents that young Chester was not a member of the Baptist faith in his adult life, and they constantly urged him to follow a Christian path. During the Civil War Chester's mother wrote to him: "Oh, that God would answer this, my prayer, that before I am taken from life, you may come out publically and confess Christ."

Chester attended the Episcopalian Church for much of his life, although he often attended other churches too. Late in his life, during a trip to St. Augustine, Florida, he attended services at the local Episcopal Church, then the old Spanish cathedral, finally finishing the Sunday at a joyous service at the black Methodist church. At that time he received a 21-gun salute from the black infantry and a deeply felt thank-you. They said, "We honor you as a lifelong friend of our people." A black youth had come 35 miles down the St. Johns river to bring Arthur a special gift—a young eagle, the symbol of American freedom.

At the age of 29 Arthur married Ellen (Nell) Herndon, a lovely girl who sang regularly in the church choir. Their first child was named William. At the age of two the much-beloved little boy died of a mysterious brain malady. A grieving Arthur wrote to his brother: "We have lost our darling boy. It came upon us so unexpectedly and suddenly. Nell is brokenhearted. I fear much for her health. You know how her heart was wrapped up in her dear boy." The next son born to the Arthurs was treated all the more tenderly for fear he might also die, but this child was strong.

During the Civil War Arthur served as quartermaster general for the state of New York, providing skillful and honest dispersal of the supplies sent from his state for the Union Army. As Arthur rose in the ranks of politics, the spoils system was very common. Men received political jobs not because of merit but rather because of their friends. It seemed to most observers that Arthur was just another politician who believed in the spoils system, and so when he became vice president on the ticket with Garfield in 1880, many reformers were disappointed. The only consolation to these people was that vice presidents were not very important and so Chester Arthur would just be forgotten.

Before Arthur took office as vice president, his beloved Nell died. His grief was overwhelming because their marriage had been a very happy one, with both devoted to one another. Arthur continued in his political work, but it seemed to many that he had lost much heart to go on.

And then, only four months after inauguration day, a thunderbolt struck. President James Garfield was shot and lay critically wounded.

"I pray God it is a mistake," Arthur cried when he was given the terrible news. Others, convinced that Arthur couldn't be an effective president, cried out with equal disbelief, "Chet Arthur as president! It can't be!"

During the tragic weeks of Garfield's death agony, Arthur waited with the nation in prayerful hope that the president would somehow survive. But then the grim word came that the valiant struggle was over and Garfield was dead. One observer wrote of Arthur: "Surely no more lonely and pathetic figure was ever seen assuming the powers of government. He had no people behind him, for Garfield, not he, was the people's choice. He was alone. He was bowed down by the weight of fearful responsibility."

Chester Arthur boarded the gloomy funeral train that carried the slain president back to Washington from New Jersey, where he had been taken in the vain hope that the sea would do him good. He was sworn in as president on Sept. 22, and he concluded a brief and emotional inaugural address with the words: "Summoned to these high duties and responsibilities, and profoundly conscious of their magnitude and gravity, I assume the trust imposed on me by the Constitution, relying for aid on Divine guidance and the virtue, patriotism, and intelligence of the American people."

As president, Arthur proved a welcome surprise to a nation that expected very little of him. Although himself involved in the spoils system as a younger man, he immediately supported reform and signed the Pendleton Act, which started a merit system for political jobs. It had been a disappointed office seeker who had killed Garfield, and many saw Garfield as a martyr to the worst effects of the spoils system. In signing the new bill to correct these abuses, Arthur paid tribute to the memory of the dead president.

Also during his presidency Arthur, who had struck a blow for black Americans in his youth, tried to gain justice for the Chinese. An anti-Chinese measure had been adopted by Congress. Arthur vetoed it, forcing the legislators to at least soften some of the terms of the legislation.

Throughout his term in office Arthur proved an honest and competent president, shocking those who had thought the worst of him.

The widower president regularly attended St. John's Episcopal Church, going across Lafayette Square with his children on Sundays. In memory of his beloved Nell he gave a window to the church and asked that it be placed on the south side of the building so he could see it from his White House quarters.

Only 51, a broad-shouldered and friendly man with elegant manners, President Arthur was widely expected to marry again. Rumors constantly spread when an unattached lady was anywhere near the White House. When a clever reporter discovered that the president was ordering fresh flowers every day, the rumors began to thicken. The bouquets were delivered to the White House and placed before the portrait of a beautiful woman! Was this possibly a lady intended to be the second Mrs. Arthur? But then the truth came out. The beautiful lady in the portrait was Nell Arthur, and the president was placing the flowers before her picture. The still-grieving President never ceased to pay this tribute to his wife.

After only about one year in office the president learned from his doctors that he was suffering from a kidney ailment that would likely shorten his life. He did not share this sad information with the public, and only his close associates knew of it. Later he contracted malaria, worsening his health still more. When he left office after finishing Garfield's term, he retired to private life.

Although far from an old man, Arthur knew he was dying. He was able to get in some fishing, a sport he dearly loved, but only about a year and a half after leaving office, he died. Private funeral services were conducted at the Church of the Heavenly Rest, where Nell had often worshiped. At the place where Chester Arthur was buried, a bronze Angel of Sorrows laying a palm branch atop a black granite sarcophagus was erected. The eulogy said of Arthur: "Good causes found in him a friend, and bad measures met in him an unyielding opponent."

Chester Arthur had not followed his father into the Baptist faith as the old preacher had hoped, but surely the kindly gentleman who always worked for the rights of minorities and was a loving husband and devoted father had expressed in his own way his Christian faith.■

TWENTY-THIRD PRESIDENT 1889-1893

9

Little Ben, the Gallant Soldier-Lawyer:
Benjamin Harrison

The delicious aroma of fresh fruit pies mixed with the fragrance of chicken and ham. Young Ben and his brothers and sisters loved coming to their grandfather's home after church on Sundays. There was the wonderful apple orchard to play in, and grandfather himself was full of marvelous stories.

"Tell me about Tecumseh," Ben begged his grandfather.

The old soldier smiled and said, "I defeated him at Tippecanoe, Ben, but he was a great man. He was a genius and a gentleman."

Ben went to the shelves of books in his grandfather's library and stared at them in wonder. There were so many marvelous fat books he didn't know which one to take down first. He especially enjoyed reading about the advertures of Ivanhoe and the Talisman.

Benjamin Harrison was a fun-loving boy who grew up in a small town in southwestern Ohio. His mother was a devoutly religious woman who urged her children to read to her from books and to talk about their studies. Sometimes in bad weather it was impossible to get to the church five miles away, but Sundays were reserved for religious practices anyway. The mornings were spent writing letters, but in the afternoon the whole family gathered to sing hymns until it was time to go to bed. All the Harrison children loved to sing and clap their hands, and to them it was the happiest time of the week. All their lives they would remember this warm and joyous custom, and it would remind them of God's love.

When Ben was a child, he heard his mother offer the same prayer every day for her children. It was, "My God bless you and keep you continually under His protecting care."

When Ben was eight years old, his grandfather was elected president of the United States. Immediately tragedy struck. The old general hero, who had been elected by the slogan "Tippiecanoe and Tyler Too," lived only one month after his inauguration. He died of pneumonia and became the president to serve the shortest term in history. With sadness Ben remembered all the happy times he had spent with his grandfather, and he became more serious about his own future.

Ben went to college even though it meant financial sacrifice for his father, who was determined that Ben should be able to rise to the height of his ability. At school Ben received many letters from his mother urging him to keep up his religious practices. One letter ended: "You don't know how thankful I feel to have such a good son and how proud I am that your teachers speak of your conduct in such high terms. I pray for you daily that you may be kept from sinning and straying from the paths of duty."

When Ben was 17, his beloved mother died. The time for him to choose a life career had come, and foremost in his mind were the words of his mother: "Earthly pleasures and hopes are empty; only the things of the spirit are really important."

Ben knew how it would have pleased his mother if he had become a minister. He was keeping company with a young lady named Carrie Scott at Miami College in Ohio, and the couple spoke of marriage.

"I cannot decide between theology, law, and physics," Ben confided to Carrie.

"You have said physics does not really appeal to you," Carrie said.

"Yes, so it is between theology and law. Carrie, the ministry is such a noble cause. The minister is God's co-worker in this glorious country of ours. His job is to encourage the disheartened, to comfort the mourner, to smooth the dying pillow, to be like a guardian angel to the people."

"You sound as if you are trying to convince yourself to follow the ministry, Ben, but is your heart elsewhere?" Carrie could see the confusion in the young man's eyes.

"I am told that lawyers are not as a rule good Christians, and it is most important to me that I am a good Christian. Yet, is it fair to denounce the entire profession because of a few dishonest men?"

"My professors at school have a low estimate of lawyers, Ben, that is true enough," Carrie said.

"Maybe there are so few good Christian lawyers because good Christians are discouraged from practicing law," argued Ben. "Perhaps just what this country needs is more Christian lawyers!"

Ben Harrison's mind was made up. He decided to become a lawyer. Soon after his marriage to Carrie, the young couple moved to Indianapolis and he opened his law practice. The Harrisons joined the local Presbyterian church, and Ben was made a deacon at the age of 24. Four years later, at 28, he became a church elder.

Carrie was very active in the church, and because of her bright and happy spirit she was able greatly to enliven the church social groups. Ben taught Sunday school and proudly gave testimony to his faith and the lordship of his Master, Jesus Christ, each week. He taught children and young adults, while Carrie took charge of the infants who were brought to church by local families. Ben's father was overjoyed by the way Ben was getting involved in church activities and he wrote: "He who wears worthily the honors of the church of Christ cannot fail to be the worthy recipient of the honors of his country. Would to God that more of our officeholders were God-fearing men!"

At the age of 29 Harrison became a colonel in the Union army and, although willing to do his duty, he was saddened at leaving his wife and family. He wrote longing letters home to Carrie, closing one with the fond hope, "If we can only be rich in the love of God and each other." During this time Carrie lost an infant at birth, and the poignant notation appears in Ben Harrison's diary that the child's coffin and grave cost $10.50.

Harrison quickly rose to the rank of brigadier general, and he served with notable gallantry in the Civil War. Because of his small stature of only five feet, six inches his men called him Little Ben. His devotion to the welfare of his troops when he led them in battle was anything but small. Even after the war he did not forget their sacrifices, and he fought for benefits for Civil War veterans.

In 1876 Harrison ran for governor of Indiana, but he lost the election partly because he never learned the art of cultivating people's friendship. Hardworking to the point of being a miser with his time, Harrison appeared cold to strangers. Those who knew him well were aware of his strong devotion to good causes such as the abolition of slavery and the welfare of the poor, but it was difficult for him to please a crowd as a politician must successfully do.

Elected to the U.S. senate in 1881, Harrison was the surprising choice of the Republicans for president in 1888. Everyone had expected the nomination to go to another man, but Harrison was nominated and elected president. He became the 23rd president of the United States, elected by the campaign song "Grandfather's Hat Fits Ben," a reminder to voters that his grandfather had also been president. This was the only time in U.S. history that the grandson of a president became president.

Harrison's beloved Carrie died in 1891, a few months before his term ended. Thrown into deep sorrow, he refused to campaign for a second term and lost. He returned to private life and continued to act as the elder of his church. The office to which he had been elected as a young man of 28 was still a primary concern of his. Nothing in Ben Harrison's busy life had ever been important enough to make him forget one warm evening long ago.

A religious revival had been in progress and all the students at Miami College were listening attentively to the preacher. Young Ben was so moved that he resolved in his heart to serve God all the days of his life. He recalled his father's words, "He that continues faithful alone will obtain the victory."

Ben Harrison had remained faithful. Another president, William Howard Taft, said of Harrison: "We have never had a man in the white house who was more conscientiously seeking to do his duty." That was Ben's character all his life, to do his duty.■

William McKinley

TWENTY-FIFTH PRESIDENT 1897-1901

10

To Walk Humbly with Thy God:
William McKinley

The small boy drove the herd of cows from pasture with the sun turning red and slipping to the horizon. It was a bitterly cold day in Niles, Ohio, and nine-year-old William's bare feet were half frozen. With seven children in the family, and business conditions in the country bad, there just wasn't enough money for the luxury of shoes. shoes.

"Hurry, William," shouted his father. He was a hardworking iron worker, a devoted Puritan, but poverty had always been his lot in life.

William found the earth where the cows had lain was still warm from their body heat. He stopped for a second and pushed his feet into the soft, warm dirt. Then he hurried on. William was already a serious boy, and he knew that everybody in the family had to work hard to survive.

From the pioneer house a gentler voice came: "Dinner is

ready, William." The boy looked at his mother with a surge of love. She was a Scottish woman, deeply religious, and filled with a warm love for her whole family.

Young William McKinley loved to listen to his mother's words as she taught her children what she considered the most important lessons of life. She said that nothing was so necessary as to live a righteous life and to make sure the members of the family love and care for one another.

When the boy was only 10, there was a religious revival held in Niles. Everybody was talking about it for days, and William was excited about going. He had never before experienced a real revival.

On the big day there were hymns sung and people clapping their hands, and a minister who talked for a long time. He had a good voice, and you could hear him up and down the valley. Finally the minister said, "Come forth, all you who will accept Jesus Christ." People began to rise and walk solemnly forward. Little William McKinley did not ask anybody what he should do. He had listened to the minister explaining about what it meant to accept Jesus as the most important Person in your life, and so he stood up and went forward to make his own profession of faith. His proud mother hoped that Willian would be a minister when he grew up, but before the boy had much chance to think about his future the United States was caught up in the violence of the Civil War. Young men from North and South were hurrying to join the military, and a stirring patriotic meeting was held in Niles.

The Twenty Third from Ohio was being formed, and William thought it was his duty to join. "It is for the cause of the Union," he told his mother, "and to end forever this cruel business of slavery!"

The 18-year-old boy was filled with strong patriotic feelings and the courage of his youth. His mother had sorrowfully watched young men all over Ohio eagerly joining up, and she expected William would go, but she wept. William assured her, "I will return to you without an injury!"

The young men who marched to war after Fort Sumter believed it would end quickly, but on bloody stalemated battlefields they learned the bitter lesson of war. William was engaged in battle at Antietam and in the Shenandoah Valley, and he was immediately repelled by the horror he saw. A generous and deeply religious youth, he was particularly saddened by the hatred he found in his companions.

William was a brave soldier, once driving a mule team into the thick of battle to bring a hot meal to men who had wearily stood days of battle with hardly any decent rations. Another time he galloped under fire to give an unsupported regiment the order to retreat. His commander, Lt. Col. Rutherford Hayes, who also became president, called him a "handsome, bright, gallant boy, one of the bravest and finest officers in the army." Although in the thick of many terrible battles, having horses shot out from under him several times, William completely escaped injury.

After the war, when McKinley spoke of his experiences, he never made those bombastic and glory-filled accounts of war common to veterans of that time. The things McKinley spoke about were evidences he had seen of Christian mercy, such as the generosity of General Grant at Appomattox, or a time he had seen a Union surgeon show great kindness to the Confederate wounded. It was not in young McKinley's heart to feel any vengeance towards the defeated South, even though no soldier had hated slavery more. He had cast his first vote for Lincoln in 1864, going into the military ambulance that served the front-line men as a voting booth.

The returning Civil War hero was now faced with choosing a career. In business he was cautious and clever, but much too generous for his own good. He saved a small sum, was asked for a loan by a friend, gave the entire amount, and was fleeced of his savings. He felt unsuited for the ministry, and finally turned to law. He set up a practice in Canton, Ohio, and was quickly successful.

As a young man McKinley was handsome, with shining gray eyes, a cheerful, warm personality, and deep compassion. His sympathy is well expressed in an incident concerning the striking coal miners of Massillon. Conditions in the mines were appalling, and the wages scarcely justified the terrible risks involved in digging the coal. Some desperately poor miners began to strike, and the strike turned into a riot. The miners were imprisoned as common criminals and, although the entire community was against them, McKinley took their case. He argued it with so much passion that he got all but one completely cleared. When friends of the miners raised an attorney's fee for the young lawyer, McKinley refused to accept it. "You need it more than I do," he said, though at that point in his career he could ill afford to work for nothing.

The people of Canton were impressed with the high moral character of young McKinley. He had learned neither smoking, drinking, nor swearing in the Army, and during his entire life he followed very high principles. In later years he advised a nephew what had been his own way of life: "Look after your diet and living, take no intoxicants, indulge in no immoral practices. Keep your life and your speech both clean, and be brave."

The young lawyer called himself a "simple country boy," and one incident illustrates just how naive about city ways he was. Unused to delicacies in food, he was invited to a reception for new lawyers where ice cream was served. In his humble pioneer home he had never tasted such a thing. He whispered very confidentially to the daughter of the hostess, "Poor Mrs. Parker. Do not tell her that her custard got frozen!" The girl sweetly explained that it was supposed to be frozen because it was ice cream.

McKinley refused to bet on the horses, because he considered this a wrongful use of money. He was, however, a superb horseman. He loved children and was a very enthusiastic participant in picnics and meetings. At all social gatherings McKinley's laughter could be heard over the voices of all others.

McKinley married Ida Saxton, and they remained a very devoted couple for their entire life together. They had two little girls, but both died young, bringing intense sorrow to the parents, both of whom adored children. Ida was so crushed by the tragedies that she became an invalid and remained so to the end of her life.

At a time in history when bigotry was common, McKinley's own gentle nature would never allow the least sign of intolerance towards others because of religious beliefs. He had friends of every religious denomination, though he was a devout Methodist himself. He always spoke of the loving-kindness of God, and his favorite hymns revealed his own generous personality. He favored "Nearer My God to Thee," "Lead, Kindly Light," "Jesus, Love of My Soul," and "There's a Wideness in God's Mercy."

The young lawyer gained widespread respect for his integrity and also for his oratory. He had a very musical voice, between a strong tenor and baritone, and this helped him in politics. He was elected to Congress in 1876 and remained there until becoming Ohio's governor in 1892. During a period of economic hardship he won the hearts of the people by providing free food for the poor.

In 1896 McKinley was elected president of the United States. His religious practices remained unchanged in his high office. He went to Washington with a favorite Bible passage foremost in his mind: "What does the Lord require of thee, but to do justly, and to love mercy, and to walk humbly with the God?" He attended church on Sundays, joined quietly in the services, always insisted on being treated like just another worshiper.

In May of 1899 Ida McKinley's health grew worse. McKinley tried to arrange his schedule to be with her as much as possible. During this time national problems grew worrisome, and the president grieved over Ida's illness. He derived strength from his Christian beliefs, saying, "My belief embraces the divinity of Christ and a recognition of Christianity as the mightiest factor in the world's civilization."

In September of 1901, in the first year of his second term, McKinley was invited to the opening of the Pan American Exposition in Buffalo, New York. Ida's health had improved somewhat, and the president was overjoyed that she could accompany him on the trip. With her at his side, he embarked on the final journey of his life.

At the exposition hundreds waited to shake the president's hand. The doors were opened, and McKinley said, "Let them come." Thousands poured through the opened doors towards the president, who had a warm smile and a firm handshake for all these strangers.

One man came forward with what appeared to be a bandage on his hand. It was, however, only a device for hiding the deadly pistol that he carried. He was an anarchist who hated all authority, and he had come to kill McKinley. He fired two shots before being wrestled to the ground by the horrified bodyguards.

Throughout the terrible moments McKinley remained surprisingly calm. As a youth in the Civil War it was noted of him that he seemed indifferent to danger. Never reckless, he just did not seem to have fear in his character. Now he remained erect, even dignified, in spite of the fatal wounds he had suffered. He said, "My wife, don't let her know of this, and if she does, don't let it be exaggerated." He saw his bodyguards dragging the assassin away, and he said, "Be easy with him boys," showing an awesome Christian forgiveness for the man who had hurt him so grievously. Finally he turned to the director of the exposition and said, "I am sorry that this should have happened at the exposition."

These were the three thoughts in the dying man's heart, concern for his wife, forgiveness for the assassin, and regret that the happy business of the exposition should be soiled by so foul a crime.

In the days that followed, there was hope that the president might recover. At times he seemed to rally. The medical bulletins then described "hope against hope." On the eighth day the president fell unconscious. He remained in a coma for seven hours. Then he awoke and whispered, "Good-bye, all, good-bye. It is God's will. His will not ours, be done."

William McKinley died as he had lived, with faith and courage. In the stirring newspaper account that appeared in the Buffalo Enquirer, Richard Barry wrote: "With that resignation in his heart, he found eternity. It was a simple, manly death—a death worthy of the president of the United States.■

Epilog

Many other presidents relied on their religious faith in times of personal and national crisis. Amidst their failures and trials it was faith in God that helped them fulfill their high responsibilities. As Theodore Roosevelt fought for such important legislation as the Pure Food and Drug and Meat Inspection laws, he could be found in church on Sundays with his large, spirited family. As a young man Roosevelt taught Sunday school in Christ Church at Cambridge, Massachusetts, and when his own daughter took up the same duties, he wrote to her: "Ethel, I am really pleased that you are going to teach Sunday school. I think I told you that I taught it myself for seven years."

Roosevelt's moral code caused him to oppose anything that he felt would weaken the family. He felt the strength of America was in its character. He read favorite passages from the Bible as well as books like <u>Pilgrim's Progress</u> to his children. Of books he said: "There is quite enough sorrow and shame and suffering and baseness in real life, and there is no need for meeting it unnecessarily in fiction." He felt that books that portray foulness should also have a joyful and noble side.

Few presidents found such exuberant joy in their children as Roosevelt found in his six youngsters. He exemplified the kind of man he felt gave strength to America: "We must have the right kind of character—character that makes a man, first of all, a good man at home, a good father, a good husband."

To Theodore Roosevelt, man had the obligation from God to be concerned with those having difficulties, the poor, the underprivileged, and his naturally warm heart fit well with this philosophy.

Andrew Jackson, at the close of a troubled life, made a formal profession of faith in the little Presbyterian church he had helped build in his wife Rachel's honor. He said he forgave all his enemies by accepting Christ, and when death was near he gathered around himself his family and friends and said, "I hope and trust to meet you all in heaven."

Many examples from the lives of the presidents could be given to show that men of politics need not be godless. Like the dying McKinley, many of them have at some time come to accept the truth that: "It is God's way. His will, not ours, be done."■